She wrote what she felt

various editions of life

Saloni Maheshwari

AF651573

BlueRose Publishers

© Saloni Maheshwari 2021

All rights reserved

All rights reserved by the author. No part of this publication may be reproduced, stored in a retrieval system or transmitted in any form or by any means, electronic, mechanical, photocopying, recording or otherwise, without the prior permission of the author.

Although every precaution has been taken to verify the accuracy of the information contained herein, the author and publisher assume no responsibility for any errors or omissions. No liability is assumed for damages that may result from the use of the information contained within.

First Published in February 2021

ISBN: 978-93-5427-510-4

BLUE ROSE PUBLISHERS

www.bluerosepublishers.com

info@bluerosepublishers.com

+91 8882 898 898

Cover Design:
Mohd. Arif

Typographic Design:
Ilma Mirza

Distributed by: BlueRose, Amazon, Flipkart, Shopclues

Poems are the kind of vibes that

convey heart to heart connection

which comes from one soul and relates to another.

-Saloni Maheshwari

Acknowledgements

I thank all who have helped me in the completion of my book in some way or the other.

Firstly, I want to thank God who gives me the ability to work.

My deepest thanks to my parents Mr.Rajesh Maheshwari and Mrs. Sunita Maheshwari who prayed for me, encouraged and supported me.

And my brothers Shubham Maheshwari and Rahul Maheshwari, without their moral support it wouldn't have been possible for me to work on my book.

My deepest gratitude and thanks to my lovely and supportive teachers, Anita Assaiya and Dr. Richa Jain who continuously motivated and pushed me in the right direction.

A special thanks to my friends Smriti Singh, Dishani Keer, Nitin Agarwal, Ayush Pandey, Yash Balwani, Aman Dahayat and Ashi Shroti who were always there for me whenever I needed their help.

Also, I would like to thank my publishers at Blue Rose and their entire team who worked with me and helped me publish my work

Introduction

Dear reader, this is Saloni Maheshwari (coco). Just a normal girl who is trying to understand the complexities of this world. Our lives are much more wonderful than lagging painfully. Every single moment can bring us joy if we have the right perspective. In this book, I have introduced the various ups & downs that a person faces in life. These are not only my beliefs but also the feelings of the people around me. Every soul in this world is unique and important; and they have their versions of life. So, this book is my version of life relating to many others'. Hope you enjoy reading my poems and connect with them.

Table of Contents

She Wrote What She Felt

Inside her heart

She tries to find herself in so many ways.

What's awry? What's straight?

So many questions were running in her head. Struggling to find her ways

For getting rid of one of the two voices from within herself;

Optimistic and pessimistic beliefs were in her head

Therefore, in the end, she started to write

What she was battling with,

What she felt inside her heart when she wasn't able to convey, she wrote what she felt

In her incompleteness, she was happy; she was unhappy

What to say and what not to?

Friends, family, relatives in her life, what to choose She was confused.

But in the end,

She started to write

She wrote what she felt...!

-Saloni Maheshwari

Nights Are My Friend

Nights are my friend.

These nights are great, they give me my room without creating any turbulence.

In the silence of the nights, I found my inner voice and peace of mind.

What I think is that these nights are made for me, so that I can give time to only myself

In the nights I cry as much as I want to because days don't allow me to

Affirm my feelings and my emotions easily

These nights help me to get inclined for a new day all over again

They give me vigour for starting my day again These nights are great

Thank you nights, for being my friend.

-Saloni Maheshwari

The Sky is Blue

The rainbow is colourful and life is so wonderful

The day starts,

With new hopes and vibes

Be the sunshine and golden sunrise from inside

Communicate positively, focus on the good

It's not only about talks

Act like you have everything you wished for

Believe and show trust 'cause God is watching over you

And you can't hide your sinful acts 'cause they capture everything.

They know you very well, 'cause nature is so beautiful

The sky is blue

The Rainbow is colourful and life is so wonderful...

-Saloni Maheshwari

She Wrote What She Felt

Do It

Do it before it's too late

Sometimes waiting goes on for life, the right time is now!

Do it now before it's too late.

-Saloni Maheshwari

Flower

Being like a flower, soft and sensitive being, I can't be hard and strong

To not go with the flow...

-Saloni Maheshwari

Your Disappearance

Felt like your disappearance won't involve anyone

Then why disappear?

Be available, and work in front of them

Let them know you are celebrating without them,

You are delighted with yourself.

-Saloni Maheshwari

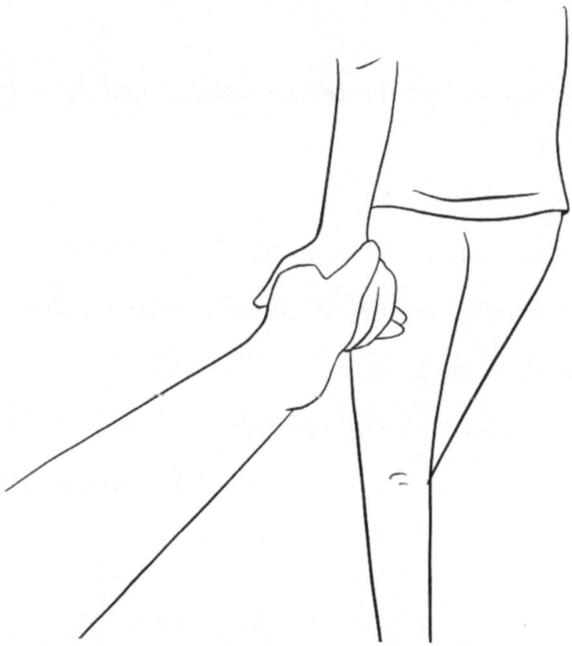

Love has no phrase

No one can replace that love

You can have a new love,

You can fall in love all over again, but you can't replace their love

You can't stop loving, it's beyond hurting and beyond remembering

The feelings are different

You want them but not in the way people understand

It's a connection of the soul, it's beyond communication

It's beyond daily meetings.

It's far away that the world can infer.

-Saloni Maheshwari

That's How I Am

Yes, I share what I feel and I can't lie

Showing my emotions for me is like avoiding my negative thoughts to pile my head

Yes, I know no one cares what you are putting on your status

they will see it and ignore it

because they are not battling from the same

The reaction will come from only those who care and think that your dilemmas are there too

Yes, I flow in emotions

If I get inclined then I will relish it, fully If I want to cry, I will cry out

I live every emotion fully and deeply so that I can understand others too.

-Saloni Maheshwari

Tired

Tired of weird eyes who gaze at me

Tired of not being apt to trust or not being trusted

Tired of having the uncertainty of travelling alone

Tired of the fact that girls can't hang out at night with their friends

Tired of not prevailing myself

Tired of that girls can't have too many male friends Everything sucks

She is free to live but still, she can't ignore where she is living

Some fights are not big, but she handles them in her daily life

Not a big issue, but she is tough enough to confront them.

-Saloni Maheshwari

She Wrote What She Felt

Male Friends

I have more male friends

It is a different kind of comfort with them, and with them, I laugh more

I hang out more, they care for me, they love me

Some are like brothers, some are like my father, some are my best friends and some like my teachers

And best of all is, they don't cheat me. They motivate me to go-ahead.

I have more male friends.

It's a different comfort zone with them, they trust me, they believe in me, they protect me

Thanks for supporting me...

-Saloni Maheshwari

Colour Black

...Black...!!!

Black is not just a colour for me

There is some sort of connection which I can't express in words

The beauty of black

Can be felt by those only who love black

-Saloni Maheshwari

Red Spots

Red stains on her skirt

She was upset about what was happening to her,

Why was this blood coming out?

She didn't know what it was.

She was in school during her first time.

She's been broken down because she was not ready for the change in her body.

That day she cried a lot because she was scared of her 'period'

Her mom told her you are now grown up

You are no more a girl; you are now a woman,

Red spots bloody days, hard to spend five days with abdomen pain, mood swings.

Till the 50s, she will be with the same

So much she is carrying all the time, being a bloody woman is not easy but I am proud to be a woman.

-Saloni Maheshwari

She's Changing

Winning over little-little challenges every day

she is changing.

-Saloni Maheshwari

Promises

Don't just promise "I am always there for you"

Learn to stick to it

Because words are powerful and your commitments can change someone's life

-Saloni Maheshwari

Mistakes

After making mistakes I came to realise that no one is going to support you because maybe you lost the trust of others. After making mistakes I came to realise that no one is going to believe in you

because once you are wrong, then that means you are wrong for forever in someone's eyes.

After making mistakes in my life, I came to realise that you will be a good person until and unless you are good going

I know I am not perfect, that's why I make mistakes.

After all, mistakes are a part of life, I learned from my mistakes.

It's good to fly high, but do not forget from where you started your life

My mistakes make me a humble being

My mistakes make me genuine

My mistakes help me learn to accept the way I am.

-Saloni Maheshwari

The feeling of emptiness

In my blank pages, there was emptiness, a hollowness

Where my thoughts are all dead and I didn't cry out,

Not even I tried to pen down from what I am going through, what can I do, where should I go, where I am

Who I am nor these thoughts were running in my brain?

The feeling of emptiness is hopeless

Nothing matters in this mental illness, neither happiness nor sadness,

The feeling of emptiness is unknown where you can't blame anyone else, not even yourself

The only way I discovered to overcome this emptiness is to keep on moving because nothing is constant so, never quit.

-Saloni Maheshwari

True Souls

Intimate your souls not your bodies.

Connect on divine levels, so no power can separate you.

Intimate your souls, not your bodies

Love is not what happens to you in class eight,

Love is a connection that happens when you meet with your soulmate.

And true feelings never die.

Time changes, feelings get deeper

You raise more, you shine up more

When you love true souls.

-Saloni Maheshwari

I Took Time

I know I took time,

I know I dropped my studies for a year, I know I took a break,

I know I spent money,

I know I got diverted from my path,

I know I was stepping on the wrong side,

But you know what?

I got to know who my true loved ones are

Who helped me to find myself all over again

I got to know the true faces of people.

-Saloni Maheshwari

Father's Love

She is praised by him, he calls her princess

She has his strong support but he never says "I love you", He simply proves it.

His actions proved me that he is the only one who loves me truly but never whispers it to me

He's my dad

-Saloni Maheshwari

No Explanations

I can't explain the reason behind what I am doing, and what I will do.

If you know me then you will never ask me those questions.

-Saloni Maheshwari

Music

To the music and the musicians

Music is therapy and musicians are therapists

They heal broken hearts and make them feel complete in themselves.

-Saloni Maheshwari

She Wrote What She Felt

I Am Hurt

It is true I'm hurt.

But, why my heart is suffering?

Why my eyes are wet?

Why I'm feeling low?

It's true I have everything in my life,

But at the same time, I feel like I have nothing.

Why my care is taken for granted?

Why my efforts are not be glimpsed by anyone?

It's true I love truly but every time I get to denial

Why won't my sentiments leave me? Why my life is getting harder?

Why I am combatting with my emotional battles? Why can't life get easy?

It's true I am tired of everything

But why doesn't anybody understand me? It's true I get furious sometimes, but nobody wants to know the reason behind it

-Saloni Maheshwari

Wandering Without Maps

When I walk alone on the streets I explore more, I absorb more

When I look at tribes and have random eye contact with them,

It makes me feel like they are mailing me some kind of message

Or maybe they want to communicate with me.

Sometimes some of them give me their company and make me smile

When I walk alone on the streets, sometimes I have fun with the dogs

When I walk alone on the streets, I don't feel lonely

Cause I am surrounded by so many things when I walk alone on the streets,

Every time there is something new, I get to learn

When I walk alone on the streets, I find so many stories

When I walk alone on the streets, I explore,

I absorb, I learn

When I walk alone on the streets, I feel free.

-Saloni Maheshwari

Pain

I am delighted to have those pains in my life which magnifies my connection with the divine.

I am pleased to have those problems in my life which turn me into a divine being from a human being.

-Saloni Maheshwari

Chasing Dreams

I am on the path of chasing dreams

But I fail to accomplish a few desires multiple times

Maybe they aren't meant for me

Or probably I have chosen something that didn't work out for me.

-Saloni Maheshwari

Passion

Feel the passion,

Find your true potential, don't get influenced by people!

Be crazy for your dreams.

Break your dreams into goals,

And achieve them step by step.

Never give up on yourself.

Just feel the passion and follow it!

-Saloni Maheshwari

What I Am from Heart

I seem like a cold person

But that's not true

Because from the heart I am very warm and soft

I look like an extrovert kind of person,

But that is not true.

When it comes to expressing my true emotions, I fail to express because I am an introvert.

Just because sometimes I don't reply, it doesn't mean I don't want to talk to you;

It simply means that I need some time for overcoming from my problems or the battle I am fighting with myself.

It is not necessary that what you predict is often true.

Sometimes, what you think can also Go FALSE so, don't judge me based on my actions and reactions.

Because it's not easy for me to open up with everyone.

Therefore, try to understand me, or if you can't,

Then don't judge me.

-Saloni Maheshwari

My Friends

I am not alone because books are with me.

The kind of friend that takes me somewhere else.

Reading a book is also a journey which I never want to end because I love travelling between the pages

And that's what helps me in imagining something new, every time.

-Saloni Maheshwari

Energy to Work

Just keep alive the pain that hurts you the most, and use that pain as your energy and work on!

The power of suffering can change your life because that gives you some reason to work on.

It works like fire that is in you,

and if you want to win, then sometimes you have to lose to win yourself.

-Saloni Maheshwari

My Dear Mother

She carries you for nine months in her body,

She feels the pain that you can't even imagine,

She fights with herself to bring you out into this world.

After your birth,

She looks after you, cares for you,

She feeds you.

You can't even count on your fingers, her unconditional love for you.

You are her whole world, her life revolves only around you.

She is a superwoman; she is your mother.

She wants to see you happy.

She hides her pain to make you happy; she doesn't leave you.

She never gets off from her work and responsibilities,

Cause she lives for you

How can you forget about her?

Don't ever get too lost in your own life, be by her side.

Just because you are a grown up and have your own home,

Don't forget about her!

She needs you.

But she will never complain about you.

She will remain silent and wait for you. All she needs is your love, care and time but she will never ask for it.

She will wait, read her silence and feel blessed that you have a mother. Some don't!

They have only memories and tears instead.

So, love her.

-Saloni Maheshwari

In the State...

When I was in the state of unconsciousness,

It's the stage when I was drunk and when I had a hangover

That means I was broken.

I was drunk because I wanted to flush out all emotions into tears;

I wanted to scream

I was tired of being in the state of consciousness What was wrong in my head?

-Saloni Maheshwari

Copy, Paste?

Why copy and paste?

Do things that make you an enormous being? Find your best

Do something that is beyond fame, go for what makes you happy.

Life is too short to waste, remember that you are unique.

So, don't copy and paste. Be what you are!

-Saloni Maheshwari

Loyalty

I may not tell the truth but trust me, I will never tell an untruth 'cause I know how badly it damages.

Specifically, when you show your faith and trust me completely,

I will stay loyal, I will stay honest, until and unless you don't cheat on me,

I will never hurt you

-Saloni Maheshwari

Love

Maybe I don't receive love in return

But I will never stop loving

-Saloni Maheshwari

Manifest

Try to manifest what you want

It gives you faith for not losing yourself

And heals you in moving on

Keeps you motivated and

It's a belief that speaks to you

You are the best

And you will have everything

In your life what are you trying to manifest

Just keep the faith.

-Saloni Maheshwari

Best Friend

Even a conversation between me and my best friend is happening less than it was happening before

Both of us don't know about each other's life

But when we meet, nothing is changed between us

Communication is the same as it used to be.

She was there when I was going through a breakdown

She wiped my tears when no one was there, she is the only one who still recognizes

What is going on in my life, without asking me.

She keeps an eye on me;

No matter how busy she is,

She will take a break from her life and hang out with me for a day

And find a way to my dilemmas

And the same things I do for her

That's why we are the best together.

-Saloni Maheshwari

Learning in Life

There is always something to learn in our lives

And it all depends on

How much we observe and listen to others, how much we understand

Every moment of life is very precious

You can't miss it,

Because the universe is always trying to teach you something Every moment of life is an event

The only difference is that Sometimes they are unplanned.

But whatever happens in our lives, there is some reason behind

The kind of vibes

That leaves a message for you.

-Saloni Maheshwari

Mother Earth

Why survive within four walls? Open your closed doors,

There is so much to examine - why to build your own home?

When you already really have your home, Mother Earth!

Save your real home; take care of it.

Plant trees,

Don't kill animals, love every one

This whole Earth and everything you have on it is yours

So, take care of your real home or very soon,

You'll have none.

-Saloni Maheshwari

Dreams...

I can sense it, people are secretly getting jealous of me and I am losing them,

Cause I am chasing my dreams.

And I don't have any regrets of losing them,

My success will show them,

Who I am!

And trust me, she will achieve everything she wishes for

Of course, she is working on her dreams

-Saloni Maheshwari

Living Alone

First, they meet you to heal you.

Then, the same person who healed you will break you
And this shit will go on

and on, because you can't live alone for whole life

-Saloni Maheshwari

We All are Same

What I truly believe is,

We all are interdependent; nothing is separated

In fact, at some point, our thoughts inter-cross and get connected.

What I truly believe is,

This universe and our souls everything

And everyone's vibes communicate.

Only the ways can be different. But overall, we all are same.

-Saloni Maheshwari

Choices

Hanging on a seesaw is what choices made me feel

It's a dilemma I can't solve easily

Complications appear with choices because

There is a sacrifice between

Either this or that,

It's like a story where you have two sides

And if I chose the one, I won't be able to see the other side

It's a feeling of incompleteness

Where you have to leave one and accept another one

In every era of life, the feud of choosing between the choices is never going to end until you are alive.

It's your choice what to choose and what not to.

-Saloni Maheshwari

Broken Heart

Her heart is broken

She articulated her creativity better than she used to perform

Now, she is glowing more.

Now, her broken heart has healed

You might never know, how she turned mature enough to be herself to live her life by being independent.

Her purpose in life is bigger than it was

You can't predict her. Now, she has grown up! And she will never share herself whole again

Her heart is broken

But still, she doesn't give up on,

Learn from her, you should be proud of her!

She is a woman.

Maybe your mother

She may be your sister or daughter...

-Saloni Maheshwari

It's Your Choice

Stay with me or stay away from me

It is Your choice

I simply don't want any shit around me

If you have a problem, then leave.

-Saloni Maheshwari

Self-love

I deserve self-love so I am loving myself. My soul needs my help,

No one else can heel, only I can do that for myself,

So, I am loving myself first, then everyone else.

-Saloni Maheshwari

Expectations?

If you keep expectations of unconditional love

Then, why don't you expect the unconditional pain in a relationship?

-Saloni Maheshwari

Nostalgia

Memories of you still live in me

And they send me in the flashback that,

Reminds me of you and makes me feel wounded in a pain, it's a flaw that flows deep

Down in my threads, it's a nostalgia

That makes you live in me

I'm moving ahead but in the back of my mind you're there or,

I'm getting used to of it, being nostalgic.

-Saloni Maheshwari

Creativity

Creativity runs in her veins and she is working on it,

Because she wants to create something remarkable.

She wants to make her name uniquely designed, her mind never goes on holiday.

And she forgets to sleep even in the nights because she prioritizes her dreams over her sleep

The creativity runs in her veins and she is working on them

So that she can get a master's in that.

Sometimes, she indulges herself into arts and sometimes in dance and music

Or in cooking food or playing a sport

Sometimes in wearing a dress,

And sometimes, in just communicating with the universe.

Due to that, the thoughts appear in her head

That's what makes her creative.

-Saloni Maheshwari

Tears

In the form of tears, it was a fear of losing.

In the form of tears, it was ignorance.

In the form of tears, it was a reaction.

In the form of tears, it was insecurity.

In the form of tears, it was a wound.

In the form of tears, it was hurt.

In the form of tears, it was depression.

In the form of tears, it was loneliness.

In the form of tears, it was failure.

In the form of tears,

There were so many reasons

Which were hard to express in words.

-Saloni Maheshwari

I cried

I cried for you in front of my friends

But whenever I met you, I pretended to smile in front of you

because I never want to make you feel bad for what you did.

-Saloni Maheshwari

Dark Circles

Dark circles under her eyes

To grin when she laughs

Embark to conceal her wounds

Like she does

Dark circles under her eyes,

To grin when she laughs

And try to fit in her complexion as nothing happened

All they bloom when she cries

Or doesn't sleep in night where she combats a nightmare

It shows her dark circles are her mates in good and bad times.

-Saloni Maheshwari

I am Leaving Now.

You are free now

I will never interrupt and ask, how are you?

Where are you? what is going on?

Why are you not picking up my calls?

Is everything all right?

You are free now

I will never tell you, please meet me once.

You are free now,

And you don't need to pretend that you want to stay,

Because I don't think you want it.

Don't be with me just because I will feel bad if you left.

Let me remind you,

I was living without you earlier also

And I can live my life once again without you

You are free now

Because I don't want to fake people in my life, and I don't want to see you again.

You are free now,

Because I don't want to love you again. Expressing love for you was my mistake.

You are free now,

Because I am leaving.

-Saloni Maheshwari

Wait

Waiting is the only destination I could ever reach,

But I failed to find you when I reached there.

And what I am feeling is a never-ending feeling. Because waiting is the only destination, I could ever reach

-Saloni Maheshwari

The Chain of Incomplete Love...

She was rejected by him for someone else

She rejected someone else for him

He broke her heart for someone else

She broke someone's heart for him

He ignored her for someone else

She ignored someone else for him

Nor he valued her love

Nor she valued someone else's love for her,

Nor he is with his love

Nor she is with her love

Nor someone else is with their love

Now all of them are left with their incomplete love.

-Saloni Maheshwari

On Social Screen

Oh wow, everything seems perfect on it

Putting on the status and posting pictures

Getting likes and comments

Oh wow, looks like they are enjoying

They are happy in their life

We all are comparing, making assumptions of others life and thinking they have a good life

It's not true what it looks like

It's not true, you never know

What a person is going through

Happiness is not what you gaze

On social screen

We all have something hidden

So next time when you start comparing, think twice,

Because it's a social life, the perfect one.

-Saloni Maheshwari

Comfort Zone

Being alone is becoming my comfort zone. As everyone has left me,

Now I have the time of my own for discovering my soul.

Being alone is becoming my comfort zone and I am getting closer to myself

There are many layers in me, like an onion

And I am reading all of them

The depth of knowing the self is full of thrill and warmth

I am glowing more than I used to because I am happy to be alone,

Because it is becoming my comfort zone and it is never-ending

Because the soul carries out so many journeys before it enters in a new body.

So, I am delighted that everyone has left me

Now, I can walk in the right path.

Being alone is becoming my comfort zone.

-Saloni Maheshwari

Guilty

The only guilt I have in my life is that why am I holding on

To something that is not going to be indistinguishable, as it was before.

The only guilt I have in my life ss that I am well aware of it.

But still, I am holding on

And it seems like it's hard to get rid of

From the contemplations that I created in my head.

The only guilt I have in my life is that I can't convey it all over again

Cause no one is interested in knowing the same story.

The only guilt I have in my life is that I know very well about it.

Yet I am making a mistake and taking the same shit in.

Why am I overthinking this?

I am getting used to of it

No, it can't be the only guilt it is more than that

This is not the end, there is more behind this

So-called guilt...!

-Saloni Maheshwari

You Are on Your Own

Let's do it by yourself, for yourself.

So what if no one believes in you, believe in yourself.

So what if no one is supporting you? support yourself.

So what if no one is helping you, help yourself.

Remember that this is your life, not others'

So, it's better to lose people instead of losing yourself.

So what if no one is your friend? you can be your friend

So what if you are all alone? enjoy with yourself.

Remember that this is your life, not others!

So, live it fully by being alive.

So, what if you are not like others?

So what if you do not have the things that others already have

So what if you are working harder than others?

So what if you get succeed late in your life?

So what if you do not have that name and fame in your life

Remember that those who are already succeeding in their lives are still not fully happy.

-Saloni Maheshwari

Creation of God

Have you ever asked yourself why you are here in this world?

What is the reason behind living this life?

Just ask yourself, why I am here?

And remember that we are the creation of God

So, whatever happens in your life,

There is a reason behind it.

So be thankful to God they gave you this wonderful life.

-Saloni Maheshwari

Soft Soul

The softest spirit gets numerous awful experiences in their life

And still, they remain the same loving person

Always giving one

Yes, they exist, because they are a divine soul.

These souls are meant to love others

To heal other souls and to help them.

-Saloni Maheshwari

Falling

Loving someone means you will start falling for losing yourself

The bitter truth is, no one wants to accept it.

-Saloni Maheshwari

Energy

Energy never dies it only gets shifted
But the energy keeps on floating
Whether it's favourable or suspicious.

-Saloni Maheshwari

Happiness

Happiness is in you

Happiness is with you

Happiness is the energy of gratitude

Happiness is a version of peace

Happiness is colourful

Happiness is a beautiful vibe

To feel the real happiness, look inside you

Explore inner you

The real happiness is in you.

-Saloni Maheshwari

Fear the Demon

The demon is an evil suffering

Which runs somewhere inside us

It's an illusion or past events

Which turned out into fear

Effects in our beingness and

Self-doubts live in us

Fear the Demon sometimes

Turns into tears

Hard to define what it feels like.

To crush fear it is hard

Because we all want security

And healing but we all

Can overcome from the Demon.

-Saloni Maheshwari

Own King and Queen

You are the king

You are the queen

So, wear the crown of self-love

You can run your world the way

You wish to be

There is a wide cosmos inside you

There is a mystery inside you

Discover them

Then you will start living

Then you start adoring yourself.

-Saloni Maheshwari

Fiery Women

She loves to play with fire, she is crazy for her desires

And passionate for her ambitions, she is unbreakable

And unstoppable, she belongs to everyone and no one.

She's a tough and wild dreamer, she won't need anyone because she lives in her way.

Don't try to cage her in your bonds or else she will leave you behind.

Her priorities are her passion and she is burning flame

She will do what she wants to do

She is mysterious and she wants to live with someone who dreams as she does.

She looks for a wider picture, she thinks in her unique way.

She is a fighter and strong

Don't try to mess up with her or you will get burned.

She doesn't give a damn to toxic people

She puts her fiery energy in work she is addicted to her dreams she keeps blooming even in the darkness

She is a fiery woman

-Saloni Maheshwari

If You Want Frequently Someone into Your Life

Then sometimes it is important to lose them

To give a break into your relationship

And have a distance from them for an interval

If you don't want to lose the freshness,

the excitement, and the happiness of your bond

Then it's important to bring a pause

in your relationship for a period because,

Too much regulatory can bring your relationship

to the end.

The end where the same person will never return

in your life.

So, it's better to bring silence for a period

And this way you will always have that person in your life. The constant one.

-Saloni Maheshwari

What the Single Soul Dream Of

I am starving for pure love, not for the flawless one

And in my veins, I want to feel the pain that cures me!

I am looking for genuine not for forever only for this life

With whom I can feel joy and also cry

I am dawdling for someone who never ignores me and in fact who adores me

I don't want any mythical commitments,

All I want is love not for forever only for this life until and unless I am alive

Someone who doesn't leave me in a lurch

I don't wish to fall into one side love

It breaks my heart

And I like It whole because I am a single soul.

-Saloni Maheshwari

Smile

Shattered into pieces?

Glue it with a smile.

Find no reason to keep it on your face

The first step towards moving ahead,

Is to smile

A cure for all the suffering

For not losing a hope

For boosting self-esteem

Helps in overcoming

The power of gleaming

The first step towards!

Bring it on,

Pass it on, the gift of life and SMILE.

-Saloni Maheshwari

In the Name Of Love

She was revealing

Her secrets to him

Because she trusted him blindly

She believed that

He is with her

Genuinely cares for her

And wants to be a part of her life

But she was mistaken and having

The false idea about him

What he was doing is playing with her feeling

In the name of love

All he wanted was her body

And when he was done

He left her.

-Saloni Maheshwari

She Dreams Of

She dreams of a life where she can live without fear

She dreams of a life where she can live without wondering about her colour complexion

She dreams of a life where she doesn't get judged by her body shape and size

She dreams of a life where she can live without wondering about what she has to wear

She dreams of a life where her intelligence is admired over her beauty

She dreams of a life where she found love not lust

She dreams of a life where she feels joy not hurt

She dreams of a life where she is treated like a queen by her man,

Above all, she hopes of heaven on earth

-Saloni Maheshwari

Into the Unknown

Walk into the unknown paths without having a clue

Flawlessly just go with the flow

Embrace the uncertainty and leave the fear behind

Be like a child, crumble your maturity

Make your life adventurous and walk into the unknown paths

Which are filled with thrill and suspense

Where you don't know what will happen next

You may fall apart and find that it's getting hard for you

You may face the darkness and feel blue

Maybe you aren't able to find any clue

And think of what to do but destiny has a better plan for you

You will overcome the problems and come up

With something new and you will love to walk into the unknown paths over and over again because after all, it's one life!

So, open your heart and live it fully.

-Saloni Maheshwar

It Hurts

It hurts when you can't express love to the one whom you want to, share what you feel for them just because you don't want to lose the person

It hurts more when you express your love to them and in return, you receive a rejection

And it ends with "we are just good friends", and then, nothing happens

It hurts even more when you crave for them, keeps on juggling for them, sometimes you want to move ahead, on the other hand, you want to wait for them, and due to that you don't look for another person

Because, you still want them back in your life.

-Saloni Maheshwari

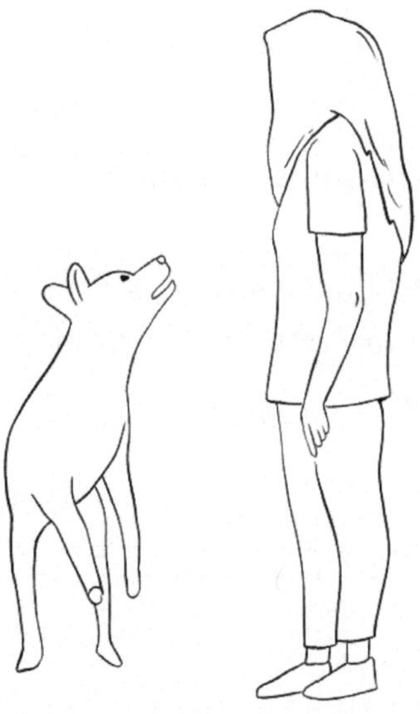

Write What You Feel, Like She Did